PATRICK MAURIÈS AND ÉVELYNE POSSÉMÉ

FAUNA

THE ART
OF JEWELRY

Photographs
Jean-Marie del Moral

Thames & Hudson

pp. 4–5
René Lalique (1860–1945)
Swallows pendant brooch
Paris, c. 1906–8
Gold, ronde-bosse enamel and counter
enamel, old-style brilliant-cut diamonds
H. 6.2 cm; W. 10.8 cm
Gift of Madame Stéphane Desmarais, 1983
Inv. 54422 A

p. 8
René Lalique (1860–1945)
Two Peacocks comb
Paris, c. 1898
Brown horn, blue and gold patina, opals
H. 18.4 cm; W. 8.6 cm
Purchased from the artist at the Salon de
la Société des Artistes Français in 1898
Inv. 8754

pp. 14–15
Necklace frontpiece
Paris, mid-19th century
Gilded silver, coloured gold, amethyst,
rubies, emeralds
H. 8 cm; W. 4 cm
Gift of Henri Vever, 1924
Inv. 24263

p. 16
Maison Paul et Henri Vever
Owl comb
Paris, Exposition Universelle, 1900
Horn, gold, transparent enamel, rose-cut
diamonds, cabochon emeralds
H. 16 cm; W. 6.5 cm
Gift of Henri Vever, 1924
Inv. 24537

pp. 22–23
Albert Duraz (1926–2004)
Owl bracelet
Lyon, 1955
Silver, cabochon garnets
H. 5.5 cm; W. 9 cm; Depth 3.8 cm
Gift of the artist, 1992
Inv. 992.579

CONTENTS

Following a volume devoted to floral jewelry from the Musée des Arts Décoratifs in Paris, we now cast our gaze over the museum's collection of jewelry inspired by animals of all kinds. Mammals and birds, real or imaginary, insects both exotic and everyday, familiar beasts from the countryside, exotic creatures from faraway lands or fantastical hybrids from the realm of dreams, the pieces showcased here were born from myth and legend, from close scientific observation and, of course, from the creative imagination of the world's greatest jewelers.

Like the realm of plants and flowers, the animal kingdom has always been one of the most popular sources of inspiration for the decorative arts, and for jewelry in particular. Some of the most enduring motifs have their origins in political or religious symbolism, drawing on the heraldic tradition. Naturalism became the dominant mode of the 19th century, an era that saw not only the founding of our museum but also a widespread renaissance in artistic practices and craft techniques and the emergence of the industrial arts. Then, in one of the pendulum swings we often see in the history of taste, the 19th and 20th century began to combine scientific and zoological knowledge with the seductive power of a new kind of symbolism that was otherworldly and sometimes unsettling.

Once more, the challenging task of selecting a hundred or so works has been entrusted to Évelyne Possémé and Patrick Mauriès, whose enthusiasm and knowledge is captured in these pages and echoed by the photographic eye of Jean-Marie del Moral.

Yet again, this book has been made possible by the involvement of the jewelry house of Van Cleef & Arpels and their training school, the École des Arts Joailliers. The house, the school and our museum are linked by a longstanding friendship, based on an ongoing dialogue between heritage, creativity and education. The lasting nature of this bond is a remarkable show of patronage and it is a pleasure to express warm thanks to Marie Vallanet and Nicolas Bos for the kindness and generosity that they always display.

Olivier Gabet
Director of the Musée des Arts Décoratifs

The publication of Fauna, a continuation of the adventure that began with Flora, is testament to the enduring collaboration between the Musée des Arts Décoratifs and the École des Arts Joailliers, which share a common goal of promoting the craft and history of jewelry-making.

Since 2015, we have been proud to support the museum's jewelry gallery and the publication of books based on its collections. The second volume in a series, Fauna echoes the characteristic style of the collection: fluent and engaging, erudite and educational, yet approachable and accessible to all. It opens the door onto an enchanting world of jeweled animals that have been humanity's companions throughout history, right up to the present day.

The desire to showcase and understand jewelry lies at the heart of our work. Passing on knowledge, lifting the veil on the secret world of jewelry and sharing it with the widest possible audience: these are the ambitions of the École des Arts Joailliers, the school of jewelry arts founded in 2012 with the support of Van Cleef & Arpels. Anyone eager to learn can discover jewelry-making and gemmology through a range of different courses, workshops and lectures, both in Paris and around the world. The school also offers special workshops aimed at children and teenagers.

The enthusiasm of the students as well as the growing public interest in exhibitions and events dedicated to applied arts and crafts are a great motivation to continue this valuable work.

Marie Vallanet
President, École des Arts Joailliers

Nicolas Bos
President, Van Cleef & Arpels

A CURIOUS
VARIETY OF FORMS

n Paris in 1808, an author calling himself G. P. Philomneste – a name suggesting a love of classical antiquity – published a hefty volume entitled *Philological Entertainments, or Curiosities of All Kinds*. Among other things, it included a 'curious poetics covering every type of verse', 'an etymological vocabulary of the different types of divination', a 'nomenclature of the song or cry of the principal birds to be found throughout the world', some 'interesting details regarding longevity and the beliefs and superstitions of some great men', a 'chronology of famous authors arranged in terms of subject matter', an 'overview of the falling value of the French *livre* since Charlemagne', a 'report on diamonds, together with a valuation table', and 'in short, numerous other items of curiosity as detailed in the list of contents'.

G. P. Philomneste was the pseudonym of Gabriel Peignot (1767–1849), who went on to publish the *Book of Singularities*, a work with even more varied content, under the same name in 1841. Like Aulus Gellius in the 2nd century, Étienne Tabourot des Accords in the 16th century, John Aubrey in the 17th century and Isaac Disraeli in the 19th century, Peignot was one of those master polymaths whose prodigious memory and indifference to the bullish generalizations and hollow syntheses that now masquerade as profundity can never be sufficiently celebrated. As well as his *Treatise on the Choice of Books* (1817), Peignot's works included *Chronological Essay on the Harshest Winters, from 396 BC to 1820 inclusive* (1821); *A Study of the Dance of Death and the origin of playing cards* (1826); *Testaments Ancient and Modern, selected for their importance, singularity or strangeness* (1829); *A Study into the Luxury of Roman Furnishings with notes* (1837) and *Predicatoriana, or Unusual and Entertaining Revelations concerning Preachers, combined with bawdy extracts from strange and witty sermons preached in France and abroad* (1841). These are just a few of more than 130 books and treatises that make up an entire library in their own right and are greatly sought after by collectors. In the words of the Larousse *Great Universal Dictionary of the 19th Century*: 'This quick-witted, cheerful, hard-working, selfless scholar compiled countless small works, most printed in limited editions, which are much sought after by the curious; they deal with intriguing and little-known facts.'

The quietly industrious Peignot is mentioned here because of a subject he discusses in *Philological Entertainments* – not diamonds, but the 'symbolism of flowers, trees, animals, colours, maps, etc.', and most specifically the third of these. This meticulous scholar records the secret meanings traditionally associated with various members of the animal kingdom, from eel to turkey cock, oyster to lizard, sparrow to viper – in these cases, misanthropy, arrogance, tranquillity, affection, melancholy and slander respectively. More famously, the bee is associated with hard work, the cat with independence, the swallow with happiness (often fleeting), the lion with strength (although when 'pierced by an arrow and eager to extract it', also with vengeance), the butterfly with fickleness, the hen with fertility, the fox with cunning, the monkey with mimicry, the bull with temperance and the dove with conjugal fidelity. The ant symbolizes thrift, but is also the subject of one of Peignot's typical asides: 'the ant is said to be the only creature that buries its dead, as man does; but this has not been proven.' Peignot couples his list with a table recording the average life expectancies of various animals, for reasons that remain unclear but are probably just a reflection of his love of digression and what Charles Fourier would have called his 'composite passion'.

Peignot's list is valuable because it pins down a set of meanings and symbols that were once widely known but now have largely been lost to us (although we might well wonder how many people ever knew that the frog symbolized curiosity, the stoat represented predestination or a 'goose holding a stone in its beak' meant silence). Some of this symbolism lives on, albeit implicitly or filtered through folk wisdom, in the world of jewelry, where, in terms of popularity, animal motifs are second only to plants and flowers.

Judging by the splendid but subjective selection displayed in the three volumes of Henri Vever's *French Jewelry of the 19th Century* (1906–8), it is clear that jewelry with animal motifs – despite some virtuoso examples – was far less common in this period than either floral or geometric compositions, since it accounts for only around forty pieces in a work of 1,300 pages. It is fair to say, however, that the 20th century helped to shift the balance. Every era is marked by its own particular tastes, and our own seems to prefer the dynamism and exoticism of animals to the Second Empire's overflowing baskets of gem-studded flowers, which now look as saccharine and old-fashioned as a painting by Winterhalter. Animal motifs proliferated in the 20th century, although their significance owes less to the immemorial qualities identified by Peignot and more to the aura generated by the fashion designers and brands that made such skilful use of them. Instead of representing ferocity, strength or wisdom, to us the panther means Cartier, the lion Van Cleef or Chanel, and the snake Bulgari.

Animals are as intrinsic to the art of jewelry as flowers, human figures and abstract motifs. Yet unlike those other forms of decoration, animals possess something primal and elemental. Rather than choosing any other subject for their paintings, including the human form – with the exception of the occasional handprint – prehistoric humans decided to depict the creatures on which they depended for their survival, yet which were also threats to that survival. Whether flying, crawling or running, minute or massive, beasts to be hunted or reared, wild or domesticated, animals were humanity's most familiar reality, and the one on which they most closely depended. Animals have always evoked an interpretative response in us, a desire to appropriate their forms and create something beautiful. We need only think of the extraordinary gold ram found in Crete in the 2nd millennium BCE or the tiny duck carved from rock crystal in the early centuries of the 1st millennium CE.

Of course, animals may also possess a symbolic, even metaphysical, dimension. One of the most obvious examples of this kind of symbolism in Western culture is the dove, which is central to the French regional style of jewelry known as 'Holy Spirit' pendants, yet at the same time has inspired couturiers such as Yves Saint Laurent and Christian Lacroix. Another is the lamb of God, which with slightly different connotations, may also recall the myth of the Golden Fleece. However, although the fish was a commonly used Christian symbol in Graeco-Roman times, and may be the basis of the little rock crystal amulet (see page 81) made somewhere in the ancient world, it has now lost much of its allegorical weight.

The snake is another creature with a clearly symbolic aspect, yet beyond its Judaeo-Christian connotations with evil, it also played a significant role in Egyptian, Greek and Latin mythology and was later the subject of obscure esoteric and alchemical symbolism. The durability of the snake as a jewelry motif is amply demonstrated by a modest gold bracelet (see page 73), which could just as easily be dated to the ancient world or to the 19th century, with its love of imitation. The serpent bracelets found on the wrists of those buried beneath the ashes of Pompeii were mirrored, centuries later, by the snakes – both ornamental and real – worn as accessories by the eccentric Marchesa Luisa Casati, prototype of the Gothic vamp during the early decades of the 20th century, who liked to parade around with a live boa constrictor coiled around her neck, her arms and fingers bedecked in matching snake-motif jewelry.

A creature both fearsome and ambiguous, linked to the powers of the underworld, emerging from the entrails of the earth but capable of reaching towards the light and possessing the potential for redemption, an attribute of oracles and priestesses, the snake merits three entries in Peignot's list of animal symbols. Although snakes traditionally represent wisdom, when two of them are wound around a staff to form a caduceus, they may also symbolize commerce. Meanwhile, a snake devouring its own tail – the ouroboros, first found in Egypt in the 16th century BCE and later adopted by many cultures and civilizations – is an image of eternity. Along with birds and butterflies, snakes are one of the most popular animal motifs for jewelry. While birds represent flight and butterflies symbolize the ephemeral, the snake embodies slowness, undulation, stretching, twisting and sinuous movement: in other words, it is naturally, intrinsically aesthetic. It even prompted the oracle of style Diana Vreeland to sing its praises, in one of the sweeping pronouncements for which she was most renowned: 'The serpent should be on every finger, and all wrists, and all everywhere!'

Patrick Mauriès

A PRECIOUS
BESTIARY

The human race has always been part of the animal kingdom, and from the very start, our lives have depended on our relationships with other animals. Our superior intelligence meant that we quickly learned to use animals for our own advantage, depending on them for food, raw materials and energy. The advent of sedentary lifestyles and the growth of cities have distanced human beings from the animal kingdom, and today wild animals are confined to zoos or held on reserves. Animals no longer inspire fear; they are no longer an immediate danger to most of us. But the further we move away from the animal kingdom, the more closely we study it, and the more we realize how necessary it is to human life. We have now become protectors of animals, even the most ferocious among them, who are now threatened with extinction. The marks of this slow evolution can be seen in human arts and crafts: the presence or absence of animals in artistic and symbolic iconography tells us a great deal about our relationship with the animal kingdom, and jewelry is particularly interesting in this respect.

Prehistoric humans had a close relationship with the animals with which they were surrounded: they had to learn about animals and face them head on, in order to feed and protect themselves. Animals were admired for their strength and humans endeavoured to take on their traits. Cave paintings depict ritualized hunting scenes with hunters wearing furs and other trophies taken from the fiercest beasts – the claws and teeth of bears, tigers and other wild cats – and images of these animals were carved into ivory or bone. Shells, coral, mother-of-pearl, feathers and leather were the raw materials for prehistoric jewelry, along with polished and painted pebbles.

In ancient Egypt, animal imagery was closely linked to religion and the cult of the Pharaohs. Jewelry made of gold, gemstones and ceramics depicts vultures with outstretched wings, as well as cobras and falcons. Baboons and cats were deified and mummified. The scarab or dung beetle, thought to symbolize the soul, played a central role in funerary rites. Wall paintings in tombs also represent idyllic and naturalistic scenes of hunting and fishing on the banks of the Nile. The jewelry of the whole Mediterranean region in ancient times was heavily inspired by Egyptian art. Mesopotamian art took a cruder, more virile approach, depicting winged bulls and lions as well as birds, while Persia's Achaemenid dynasty popularized the griffin and other fantastical creatures. In ancient Greece, bees and birds – hens, cockerels, doves and swans – appeared alongside goddesses and winged female figures as decorative devices for earrings. Snakes inspired the shape of bracelets and rings, while the heads of rams, lions and winged horses adorned the ends of bracelets and torcs. The Etruscans were excellent goldsmiths and decorated their jewelry with tiny animals – horses, lions, dolphins, antelopes – rendered in gold filigree work. Like the cylinder seals from the Middle East, the cameos and intaglios of the Greek and Roman worlds depict an entire bestiary of creatures that could be naturalistic or fantastical, drawn from myths and legends. The gods and goddesses of Olympus were associated with specific animals – Jupiter with the eagle, Juno with the peacock, Venus with the dove and the swan, Diana with the owl – each of which was meant to reflect the qualities or personality traits attributed to that deity.

At the frontiers of the Mediterranean world, barbarians and nomadic peoples made jewelry in which animals reigned supreme: the figures of horses and deer studded the creations of the Hittites (3000 BCE), the Hyksos (1730 BCE), the Scythians (5th century CE) and, closer to home, the Celts. During the High Middle Ages, the Merovingians created jewelry covered with garnets and enamel and took inspiration from the forms of eagles and other birds, as well as cicadas. In Byzantium, birds were also a familiar motif on imperial costumes and textiles.

During the Middle Ages, animals did sometimes appear as decorative motifs in church interiors, sometimes to the displeasure of clergy who believed them to have heathen connotations, but scarcely any animal motifs are found in the jewelry of the period. The Church had by then begun trying to distance man from his primitive instincts, which conflicted with religious ideas of virtue. The many bestiaries produced at this time were less interested in representing scientific facts than moral, religious and symbolic truths. Animals and the qualities attributed to them were intended to serve as models to good Christians. While endeavouring to classify real-life animals – wild and domesticated beasts, birds, fish and other water-dwellers, snakes and worms – the authors also incorporated fantastical creatures into these works. For instance, the dragon was genuinely thought to exist and was regarded by medieval man as the king of serpents. In jewelry, animals only featured as attributes of saints, as symbols of the Evangelists or in reference to stories from the Old or New Testament: the dove and the raven from the tale of Noah; the ram sacrificed by Abraham; the golden calf of the Israelites; the bronze serpent made by Moses; the bear and the lion slain by the young David; Tobias's dog and fish; Daniel and the lions; Jonah and the whale; and several others.

The 16th century and the Renaissance were a period of genuine scientific study into the animal kingdom. Discoveries were made regarding the different stages of insect metamorphosis. In the field of jewelry, the use of baroque pearls gave rise to an extraordinary array of pendants that made use of the irregular shapes of the pearls to portray all manner of creatures, both real and fantastic: salamanders, lizards, cockerels, pelicans, winged horses, fishes and dolphins, mermaids, dragons and sea monsters. Some of these – such as the mystic lamb – have clear religious connotations. Others are imbued with a different sort of symbolism. The pelican, for instance, is often featured in portraits of women as a symbol of maternal love, because it was believed to feed its young with its own blood.

During the 18th century, the Swede Carl Linnaeus and the French Comte de Buffon established the great systems of animal classification that form the basis of our current knowledge of natural history. Despite this period of intense scientific research, however, the animal kingdom was kept at bay in artistic circles, being rarely represented in the decorative arts and even less so in jewelry.

In the early 19th century, the Empire wanted to renew its ties with classical art. Napoleon Bonaparte chose the eagle of ancient Rome and the bee of Emperor Charlemagne as emblems of his rule, while the Empress Josephine favoured the animal attributes of Venus and Cupid: the dove, swan and butterfly.

The Romantic era cast its gaze back to the figures of the Middle Ages: beautiful women mounted on their palfreys, setting off for the hunt with a falcon on their wrist. During the second half of the 19th century, the rediscovery of the decorative arts in France and of the albums of decorative engravings published by Étienne Delaune and Pierre Woeiriot led to a new wave of interest in the fantastical creatures that these Renaissance artists created. At the Expositions Universelles in 1878 and 1889, French decorative artists adopted an eclectic range of approaches but with a particular focus on the work of Renaissance goldsmiths. Jewelry designers like Alphonse Fouquet, Frédéric Boucheron, Émile Froment-Meurice and Louis Wièse drew inspiration from it, recreating fantastical creatures set on either side of figures in painted enamel. The monsters dreamt up by Chinese and Japanese artists further enriched this extraordinary menagerie, whose creative exuberance was matched by the quality of the metal tooling and chasing on show.

This imaginative iconography was continued, albeit in a more serene style, by Art Nouveau. Drawing on the pantheist vision of nature embraced by Henri de Régnier and other Symbolist poets, artists such as René Lalique, Henri Vever and Georges Fouquet created jewelry depicting women's heads with butterfly or bird wings, a snake rearing up from a naiad's forehead, and a mermaid forming the body of a bronze comb decorated with carved opals. These flower women and insect women reflect a world caught up in a process of transformation: when animals are no longer familiar sights in everyday life, mankind once again turns for inspiration to the wildness and mysteries of nature.

During the first half of the 20th century, a handful of striking pieces – Cartier's Asian-inspired panther, for instance – proved that animals were still a good subject for jewelry; but it was not until the 1950s and 1960s that they became omnipresent motifs once again. Great jewelers like Jean Schlumberger and Fulco di Verdura created a gem-studded bestiary to rival the creations Schlumberger had conceived for the couturière Elsa Schiaparelli before the war. Jewelry drew on a new source of inspiration – the world beneath the waves. Fish, sea urchins and starfish set with precious stones blossomed from jacket lapels, while in Lyon, Albert Duraz invented a panoply of fantastical armour-plated creatures that seem to foreshadow the 'gothic' style. It was also around this time that the house of Van Cleef & Arpels opened La Boutique; among its offerings was a range of charming animal clips featuring a floppy-eared dog, a tousle-headed lion and a mischievous kitten. Every year, the firm launches a new jewelry collection in which naturalism and fantasy both play a role: in 2007, the Atlantide collection explored the theme of ocean life; in 2010, Les Voyages Extraordinaires took their inspiration from the works of Jules Verne; and in 2016, the Noah's Ark collection introduced pairs of jeweled animals and birds.

Animals have been part of our world since the dawn of time. We have embraced, exploited and tamed them, but they are also a part of ourselves. Wild or domesticated, real or fanciful, they feed our imaginations. Humanized by mythology, in stories and legends by the likes of Charles Perrault, Jean de La Fontaine and Jean Cocteau, they are our mirrors, a reflection of our own souls. Now that animals are more widely recognized as living beings with rights and no longer as mere objects, the hope persists that humanity will learn to protect the world from which we have tried to distance ourselves, whose most natural and noble denizens are now at risk of vanishing forever.

Évelyne Possémé

CREATURES
of the AIR

Birds are generally seen as
having positive symbolic
associations and they
traditionally acted as messengers
between humanity and the gods.
Their lofty home in the heavens
makes them seem far removed
from earthly contingencies
and closer to the realms of the
spirit. While highly regarded in
the Islamic world, bird motifs
are less significant within
Christianity, with the exception
of the dove, symbolizing the
Holy Spirit, and the eagle
associated with St John. A bird
may also be a metaphor for
our aspiration to rise above our
earthly condition, as illustrated
by the Icarus myth – a warning
against pride and the desire to
flout the limits imposed
on humanity by the gods.

Opposite and right:
Pair of earrings
Italy, antiquity
Gold, amethyst beads
H. 3.2 cm; W. 3 cm
Bequest of Jeanne-Marie Mosticker, 1966
Inv. 40347

Doves and pigeons – the birds of the Columbidae family – have been associated with love and romance since ancient times. The dove was the sacred bird of Aphrodite in Greece and of Venus in Rome. In the 18th century, these birds symbolized married love, because it was believed that they mated for life. The inscription on the Chantilly porcelain pendant means 'Let us imitate them'; similar mottoes can be found on many pieces of jewelry with the same motif, from Britain as well as France. Swans – which are associated with Apollo – are sometimes shown pulling the chariot of Venus in place of doves. The 'Swan of Love' is a play on words in French, based on the similarity of *signe* (sign) and *cygne* (swan), a pun often found in medieval texts.

The motif of a pair of birds on a branch or in a nest was popular in French jewelry of the period 1830–50. A symbol of conjugal love, it was also used to express love of family and home and the care of infants, as represented by the eggs or baby birds in the nest. This motif was very popular when interpreted by the jeweler Simon Petiteau, and was subsequently used by Jean-Charles Morel, François-Désiré Froment-Meurice and Frédéric-Jules Rudolphi.

Below:
Maison Morel et Cie (1842–48)
Jean-Baptiste Klagmann (1810–67), sculptor
M. Milleret, engraver
Bracelet maquette
Paris, 1842–48
Gilded and silvered metal, imitation pearls
Diam. 7 cm; W. 4 cm
Gift of Jules Brateau, 1901
Inv. 9503 A

Opposite:
François-Désiré Froment-Meurice (1802–55)
Jules Wièse (1818–90), jeweler
Birds pendant brooch
Paris, c. 1839
Gilded silver, transparent enamel on a guilloché ground, mother-of-pearl, pearls
H. 9 cm; W. 5 cm
Gift of Henri Vever, 1924
Inv. 24382

A symbol of power since ancient times, the eagle was the emblem of the Roman Empire, the Carolingian Empire and the Holy Roman Empire. Napoleon used it in the form of an eagle clutching Jupiter's thunderbolt in its talons. René Lalique's pendant is a reference to a play by Edmond Rostand entitled *L'Aiglon* (*The Eaglet*), which was based on the life of Napoléon II, son of Napoleon Bonaparte and the Empress Marie-Louise. Sarah Bernhardt, who played the title role when the play premiered on 15 March 1900, acquired the pendant at the Exposition Universelle in the same year, and presented it as a gift to the poet Rosemonde Gérard, wife of Edmond Rostand. Madame Rostand is shown wearing the pendant in a drawing by Jules Pascin housed in the Villa Arnaga, which is now the Edmond Rostand Museum.

It was via Art Nouveau and Japonisme that the crane first became a Western jewelry motif in the late 19th century. Able to live for nearly a thousand years, according to Japanese legend, the crane is a symbol of longevity and – along with the carp, the wave and Mount Fuji – was one of the Japanese motifs most frequently borrowed by European decorative artists. The belt buckle by Charles Boutet de Monvel is a perfect example of a motif being adapted to fit a form, following the precedent of Japanese sword guards. By using the Tau Cross as a basis for his pendant, René Lalique is openly referencing Christian iconography, in which the crane represents the Resurrection because of the way it returns every spring.

Above:
Charles Boutet de Monvel (1854–1940)
Crane belt buckle
Paris, c. 1902
Silver
H. 8 cm; W. 8.8 cm
Purchased, 1991
Inv. 991.1090

Opposite:
René Lalique (1860–1945)
Cranes pendant
Mould-pressed, relief-carved
and frosted glass, with woven silk cord
H. 4.7 cm; W. 5.4 cm
Gift of Madame Crépy-Carnot, 1981
Inv. 47737

Since ancient times, the dove has been depicted on tombs and burial monuments, as a symbol of the soul ascending to paradise. The antithesis of the raven in the Christian tradition, it is mentioned several times in the Bible: for Noah, the dove was a symbol of peace and hope; for David, it represented escape and peace, while the dove of the Holy Spirit carries connotations of hope. In the New Testament, the Holy Spirit descends from heaven in the form of a dove when Jesus is baptised by John the Baptist. In the 18th and 19th centuries, the dove of the Holy Spirit was widely depicted both in jewelry and in folk contexts as a symbol of Christian faith and hope, sometimes bearing the olive branch carried by Noah's dove.

In the West, bats have often been viewed in a negative light and associated with the Devil, but in ancient China the bat was a symbol of good fortune. In the late 19th century, the bat became associated with gay and lesbian circles, perhaps because it comes out at night, or because it possesses traits of a bird and a mammal combined, thus representing androgyny. There is little doubt that this is how we should interpret the motif of these two pieces designed by René Lalique and given by the courtesan Liane de Pougy to her lover, the poet Natalie Clifford-Barney. The colour of the enamel and the moonstones was an allusion to Clifford-Barney's blue eyes.

Above:
René Lalique (1860–1945)
Bat ankle bracelet
Paris, c. 1898–99
Gold, transparent enamel on gold,
transparent paillonné enamel,
old-style brilliant-cut
and rose-cut diamonds, opals
H. 5.5 cm; L. 20 cm
Gift of Laura Dreyfus-Barney in memory
of her sister Natalie Clifford-Barney, 1966
Inv. 40100

Opposite:
René Lalique (1860–1945)
Bat ring
Paris, c. 1899
Inscription inside the ring: 'I love how you
strive to understand and love me. L.'
Silver, gold, transparent enamel,
cabochon moonstone
Diam. 1.9 cm; W. 1.2 cm
Gift of Laura Dreyfus-Barney in memory
of her sister Natalie Clifford-Barney, 1966
Inv. 40105

In Western folklore, the peacock represents vanity, pride and luxury, while in China it personifies beauty and nobility. When the decorative arts of Asia and the Islamic world were rediscovered in the late 19th century, the peacock found its way back into the Western bestiary. The colourful beauty of its plumage lends itself marvellously to the palette of René Lalique – a virtuoso in both enamelling and goldwork, with his gold jewelry being perfectly tooled on both sides. The brooch fitting of this piece can be removed, allowing the peacock to be displayed as an objet d'art.

René Lalique (1860–1945)
Peacock brooch
Paris, c. 1899
Tooled and engraved gold, enamel over gold, cabochon moonstones.
H. 2.6 cm; Diam. 6 cm
Purchased from the artist at the Salon de la Société des Artistes Français, 1899
Inv. 9076

The artist Georges Braque began incorporating birds into his work in 1949 and continued to draw heavily on this motif for the rest of his life, using a variety of techniques. Fascinated by the art of ancient Greece, he used simplified forms inspired by the gods and goddesses of classical mythology in both his paintings and his jewelry designs. The techniques and materials selected – granulated gold, jasper, fire opal – were the result of Braque's close collaboration with the jeweler Heger de Löwenfeld.

Above left:
Georges Braque (1882–1963)
Heger de Löwenfeld (1919–2000), jeweler
Hemera clip
Paris, c. 1962
Gold, fire opal, brilliant-cut diamonds
H. 4.1 cm; W. 5.2 cm
Deposited by the Centre National des
Arts Plastiques, Ministère de la Culture
et de la Communication, 1987
Inv. FNAC 1158

Above right:
Georges Braque (1882–1963)
Heger de Löwenfeld (1919–2000), jeweler
Icarios clip
Paris, c. 1962
Gold, jasper, brilliant-cut diamonds
H. 4.5 cm; W. 4.8 cm
Deposited by the Centre National
des Arts Plastiques, Ministère de la
Culture et de la Communication, 1987
Inv. FNAC 1162

Opposite:
Georges Braque (1882–1963)
Heger de Löwenfeld (1919–2000), jeweler
Asteria clip
Paris, c. 1960–62
Gold, navette-cut diamond
H. 8 cm; W. 8 cm
Deposited by the Centre National
des Arts Plastiques, Ministère de la
Culture et de la Communication, 1987
Inv. FNAC 1164

Jeweled
INSECTS

With the exception of the ceramic art of Bernard Palissy in the 16th century, insects were not popular motifs in Western iconography until the popularization of Japanese art in the late 19th century. When enlarged, these tiny creatures can seem fantastical and even unsettling. Art Nouveau jewelers often merged insects and female figures, depicting metamorphic forms such as the dragonfly woman of René Lalique and the butterfly woman of the Maison Vever, shown here. The window enamel and diamonds of the woman's diaphanous wings vie with the opaque enamel of her gown with its eye-like markings, while the transparent white agate of her upper body contrasts with the two rubies that form a heart shape on her bodice, and the butterfly antennae of her head-dress curl to form a large suspension ring.

Below and opposite:
Maison Paul et Henri Vever
Sylvia pendant
Paris, Exposition Universelle, 1900
Gold, agate, window enamel, rubies,
old-style brilliant-cut diamonds
H. 12 cm; W. 6.5 cm
Gift of Johanny Peytel, 1917
Inv. 20715

Opposite:
Heart and Butterfly pendant
Paris (?), Bourbon Restoration
Repoussé, engraved, matt and
polished gold, pink topaz and cabochon
turquoises, crystal, with a lock
of hair inside
H. 2.5 cm; W. 1.5 cm
Bequest of Jean-Jacques Reubell, 1934
Inv. 30665 E

Above left:
Julien Duval and Georges Leturcq
(active in Paris from 1885 to 1894)
Butterfly brooch
Paris, c. 1889
Gold, matt and transparent paillonné
enamel, rose-cut diamonds mounted
on silver, cabochon garnets
H. 2.5 cm; W. 3 cm
Gift of Henri Vever, 1924
Inv. 24500 A

Above right:
Alexis Falize (1811–98)
Antoine Tard, enameller
Butterfly pendant
Paris, c. 1869
Gold, opaque cloisonné enamel
H. 3.2 cm; W. 3 cm
Gift of Henri Vever, 1924
Inv. 24461 B

The butterfly is a universal symbol of grace and ephemeral beauty. In classical mythology, butterfly wings were an attribute of some nymphs, including Psyche. During the First French Empire, when neoclassicism was in vogue, the butterfly was associated with love, and during the Bourbon Restoration it could be found on pendants, sometimes perched on a heart-shaped locket holding a portrait of the beloved or a lock of their hair. In the 19th century, butterfly motifs were initially associated with Japonisme, but they were later interpreted in a more naturalistic style in both gemstone and enamel jewelry.

Below:
René Lalique (1845–60)
Grasshoppers brooch
Paris, c. 1913
Gold, mould-pressed and patinated glass
H. 3.3 cm; W. 9.2 cm
Purchased from the artist, 1913
Inv. 19292

Right:
René Lalique (1845–60)
Sloe Berries and Wasps brooch
Paris, c. 1904
Gold, moulded and patinated glass,
enamel
H. 4.7 cm; W. 11.2 cm
Gift of Madame Stéphane Desmarais, 1983
Inv. 54422 B

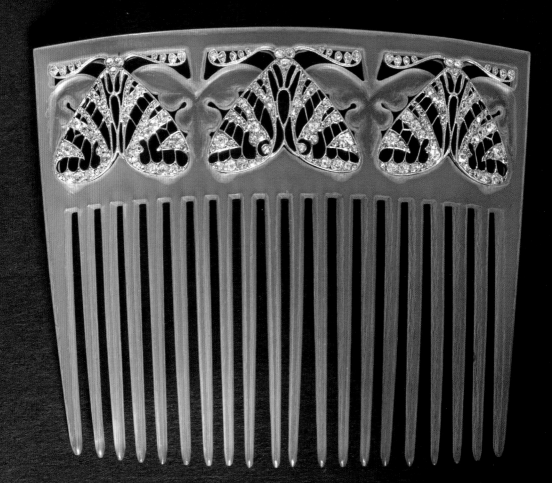

Opposite, above:
Maison Van Cleef & Arpels
(founded in 1906)
Junichi Hakose, lacquer artist
Takarasukushi O clip
France and Japan, 2008
Gold, mother-of-pearl, gold lacquer,
brilliant-cut diamonds
H. 4 cm; W. 5 cm
Gift of Van Cleef & Arpels, 2008
Inv. 2008.128.1

Opposite, below:
Maison Paul et Henri Vever
Moths comb
Paris, 1906
Horn, platinum, brilliant-cut diamonds
H. 10 cm; W. 11.5 cm
Gift of Henri Vever, 1924
Inv. 24539

Below left:
Van Cleef & Arpels
Two *Butterfly Between The Finger* ring
Paris, 2016
Rose gold, mother-of-pearl, diamonds
H. 2 cm; W. 3.5 cm
Gift of Van Cleef & Arpels, 2017
Inv. PR 2017.61.1

Below right:
Van Cleef & Arpels
Butterfly clip
Paris, 2000
Yellow gold, mother-of-pearl, diamonds
H. 5 cm; W. 4 cm
Gift of Van Cleef & Arpels, 2017
Inv. PR 2017.61.2

Butterflies were a favourite motif of Art Nouveau. Taking inspiration from Japanese prints (in the case of Alexis Falize) or scientific illustrations, artists carved butterflies and moths from horn or tortoiseshell. Their wings and antennae lent themselves to light, airy pieces whose forms could be naturalistic (Vever) or more stylized (Vever, Hamm). Today, Van Cleef & Arpels are still producing jewelry in the Japoniste style, including butterfly brooches whose lacquer work is created by Japanese craftsmen.

Grasshoppers, cicadas and dragonflies are symbols of fragility and ephemerality. Their small size, their delicate colours and the intricate patterns of their wings require the jeweler to work on a diminutive scale and with great precision, creating depictions that are often naturalistic. The dragonfly in particular became a leitmotif of Art Nouveau. The *Cicadas* comb shows the insects in high relief, their dainty wings lending themselves particularly well to the use of window enamel, which allows light to pass through like a stained-glass window. In the *Grasshoppers* comb, made of carved tortoiseshell, the bodies of the two insects meet along the vertical axis of the piece.

Above left:
Georges de Feure (1868–1943), designer
For L'Art Nouveau de Siegfried Bing
Grasshoppers comb
Paris, c. 1902
Carved blonde tortoiseshell
H. 7.5 cm; W. 10 cm
Gift of Marcel Bing, 1908
Inv. 15279 B

Above right:
Paul-Frédéric Follot (1877–1941)
Dragonfly comb
Paris, c. 1905
Horn, gilded and patinated silver,
cabochon sapphires
H. 8 cm; W. 12 cm
Purchased from the artist at the Salon
de la Société des Artistes Français, 1905
Inv. 12045

Opposite:
Gaston Chopard (1883–1942)
Cicadas comb
Paris, Salon de la Société des Artistes
Français, 1903
Gold, tortoiseshell, enamel on gold,
window enamel, natural pearls
H. 15.1 cm; W. 9.5 cm
Gift of Madame Gaston Chopard, 1952
Inv. 37291

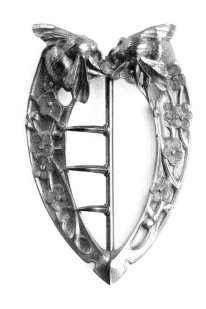

Opposite, from top to bottom:
Fly tie pin
Paris, late 19th century
Gold, baroque pearl, platinum, old-style
brilliant-cut diamonds, rubies
L. 9.5 cm; fly H. 1.7 cm; W. 1.7 cm
Spell Bound tie pin
Enamelled gold
L. 8.6 cm; head H. 2.1 cm; W. 1.8 cm
Gifts of Count Moïse de Camondo
in memory of his father Count Nissim
de Camondo, 1933
Inv. 28870 A and 28875 B

Bee brooch
Paris, late 19th century
Cast and engraved gold
H. 4 cm; W. 3.5 cm
Naturalistic Fly tie pin
Steel, patinated copper,
synthetic material
L. 7.5 cm; fly H. 1 cm; W. 0.8 cm
Bequests of Jacques Reubell, 1934
Inv. 30589 and Inv. 30643 A

Maison Paul et Henri Vever
Cicada tie pin
Paris, c. 1900
Gold and enamelled copper
H. 8.6 cm; W. 1 cm
Gift of Henri Vever, 1928
Inv. 26726

Above right:
Maison Paul et Henri Vever
Hornets belt buckle
Paris, 1907
Gold, enamel, rose-cut diamonds
H. 8 cm; W. 5.3 cm
Gift of Henri Vever, 1928
Inv. 24534

Prehistoric humans are known to have collected honey from bees and there is evidence of bee-keeping in Egypt dating from 2600 BCE. Symbols of tireless industry, these sociable, intelligent, organized and hard-working insects have been viewed as examples of model behaviour since antiquity. Art Nouveau – influenced once again by Japanese art – generally treated flies, beetles and wasps in a naturalistic manner, sometimes creating a strikingly life-like effect, an approach seen throughout the history of painting, and later revived by artists including François-Xavier and Claude Lalanne.

René Lalique (1860–1945)
Bumble Bee bodice ornament
Paris, c. 1905–6
Gold, moulded and engraved glass,
enamel, old-style brilliant-cut diamonds
H. 6 cm; W. 15 cm
Purchased from the artist at the Salon
de la Société des Artistes Français, 1906
Inv. 12745

The scarab beetle was considered sacred in ancient Egypt and when a body was mummified, a carved beetle was placed on the dead person's heart to ensure safe passage into the afterlife. The scarab motif was also embraced by the Phoenicians, Carthaginians, Greeks and Etruscans throughout antiquity, serving as a seal or a protective amulet. It was sculpted from various materials, including hardstones such as carnelian and jasper and also Egyptian faience. Produced in vast quantities, and reproduced for tourists visiting the Middle East, carved scarabs were known in the West from the end of the 18th century and popular throughout the 19th.

Above left:
Frédéric Boucheron (1830–1902)
Louis Rouvillois, jeweler
Scarab Beetle tie pin
Paris, 1878
Gold, silver, sapphire, rose-cut diamonds
Gift of Count Moïse de Camondo
in memory of his father Count Nissim
de Camondo, 1933
Inv. 28869 B

Above right:
René Lalique (1860–1945)
Scarab Seal pendant
Paris, c. 1899–1901
Gold, green jasper, enamel on gold,
black glass
H. 3 cm; W. 3.8 cm
Gift of Carle Dreyfus, 1947
Inv. 35814

Opposite:
Castellani
Scarab brooch
Rome, c. 1870
Gold, soapstone, mosaic glass
H. 2.2 cm; W. 9.1 cm; Depth 1.3 cm
Bequest of Madame la Baronne
Nathaniel de Rothschild, 1901
Inv. 9827

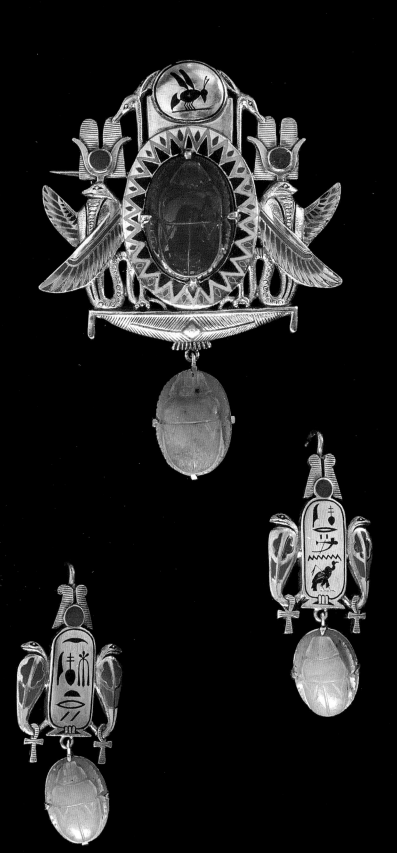

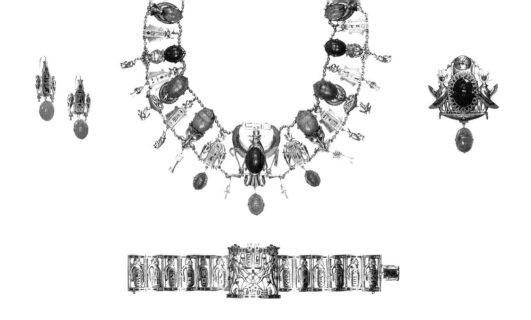

Above and opposite:
Émile Philippe (1834–c. 1880)
Egyptian-style parure comprising
necklace, bracelet, brooch and earrings
Paris, Exposition Universelle, 1878
Gilded silver, jasper, amethyst,
hardstones
Necklace: L. 43 cm; W. 6.5 cm
Bracelet: L. 18 cm; W. 3.8 cm
Brooch: H. 6.8 cm; W. 5.1 cm
Earrings: H. 4.7 cm; W. 1.8 cm
Gift of the artist, 1878
Inv. D 21

Egyptian art has always been
popular in the West and this
interest has been regularly
reawakened throughout history.
When the Luxor obelisk was
erected in Paris's Place de la
Concorde in 1833, France saw a
sudden proliferation of jewelry
adorned with pseudo-Egyptian
motifs. The opening of the Suez
Canal in the presence of the
Empress Eugénie in 1869 also
sparked a revival of interest in
Egyptian-style jewelry decorated
with hieroglyphs and scarabs.

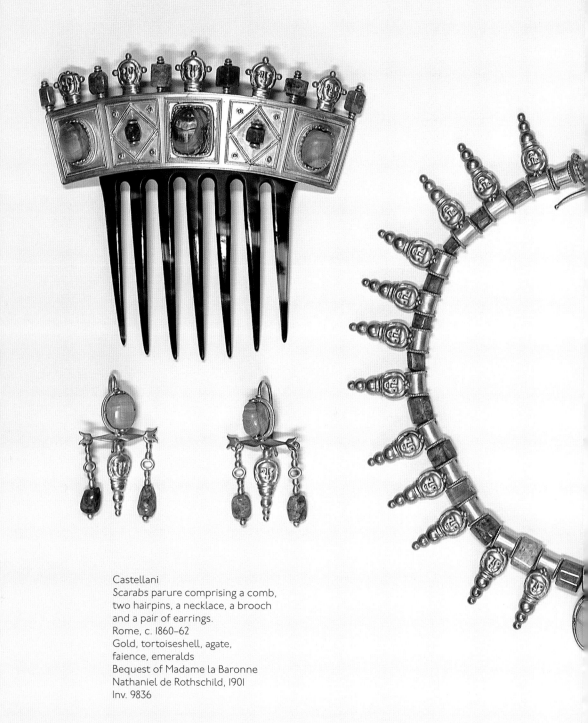

Castellani
*Scarabs parure comprising a comb,
two hairpins, a necklace, a brooch
and a pair of earrings.*
Rome, c. 1860–62
Gold, tortoiseshell, agate,
faience, emeralds
Bequest of Madame la Baronne
Nathaniel de Rothschild, 1901
Inv. 9836

SEAS
and OCEANS

The underwater world, especially the open sea, was a source of fear in ancient and medieval times. The shoreline was not seen as a place to linger and the riches of the oceans were as yet unknown. It was not until the 16th century that the sea came to be understood as a source of life rather than a place of death. By the end of the 19th century, the firm of Boucheron was regularly using pierced steel to create pieces like this *Turtle* tie pin, made by the craftsman Louis Rault, whose workmanship is exceptional.

Right and opposite:
Frédéric Boucheron (1830–1902)
Louis Rault (1847–1903), sculptor
Turtle tie pin
Paris, 1879
Gold and pierced steel
L. 9 cm; head H. 3.5 cm; W. 2.1 cm
Gift of Count Moïse de Camondo
in memory of his father Count Nissim
de Camondo, 1933
Inv. 28876 C

The fish was an early Christian symbol, its significance associated with the fact that the Greek word for fish, *ichtus*, spelled out the initials of the words *Iesous Christos Théou Uios Sôter* (*Jesus Christ, Son of God, Saviour*). In France under the Ancien Régime, many crafts and trades were regulated by guilds, whose members often wore rings stamped with the symbol of their trade: a fleur-de-lis for goldsmiths and silversmiths, a pair of scissors for drapers, and a fish for members of the fishermen's guild. The motif of the carp – in Asia, a personification of courage, strength and endurance – was introduced into Europe via Japanese art during the latter half of the 19th century. Used in Japanese textiles, stencils and embroideries, it was embraced by Art Nouveau and was used as a motif by Lalique.

Shells were popular motifs in ancient Greece and Rome but less so in medieval times, with the exception of the scallop shell, which became a symbol of the Santiago de Compostela pilgrimage route. They later re-emerged in the still lifes of the Renaissance and were revived once again by Art Nouveau, most notably in the works of the sculptor and jeweler Henri Nocq, whose idiosyncratic repertoire included them alongside seaweed, crabs and gemstones in pieces made of cast and tooled silver.

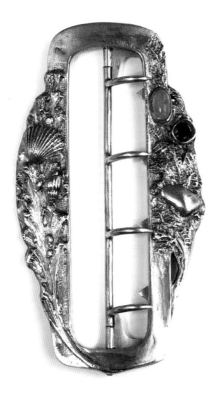

Left:
Henri Nocq (1868–1942)
Seashells belt buckle
Paris, c. 1905
Cast and tooled silver, opal, beryl
H. 11 cm; W. 6 cm
Gift of Max Polack in memory
of Henri Nocq, 1943
Inv. 35115

Opposite:
Henri Nocq (1868–1942)
Crab ring
Paris, 1897
Silver, gold, opal
Diam. 2.1 cm; W. 2.6 cm
Gift of Max Polack in memory
of Henri Nocq, 1943
Inv. 35113

René Lalique (1860–1945)
Fish bodice ornament
Paris, c. 1903–5
Enamel on gold, moulded, engraved
and partially enamelled glass
H. 6.5 cm; W. 16 cm
Gift of Laura Dreyfus-Barney in memory
of her sister Natalie Clifford-Barney, 1966
Inv. 40099

Following their low-key revival in the decorative arts of the early 20th century, fish and other marine motifs played a greater role in the jewelry of the 1950s and 1960s, with artists from both Europe and America drawing heavily on the theme. American jeweler Fulco di Verdura (an Italian by birth) created seashell jewelry, and in Paris and New York, Jean Schlumberger reproduced fish, starfish and sea urchins in gold set with precious stones. Maison Boivin and Suzanne Belperron extended the repertoire to include seaweed, mermaids, sea horses and dolphins, and Jean Lurçat used iridescent blue-tinged metal to emulate the scales of fish, alongside seaweed forms in engraved gold.

Above:
Jean Schlumberger (1907–87)
for Tiffany, New York
Fish clip
Paris and New York, 1956
Gold, amethysts and brilliant-cut aquamarines, cabochon rubies, red lacquer
H. 4.6 cm; W. 6.4 cm
Anonymous gift, 1996
Inv. 996.66.1

Opposite:
Jean Lurçat (1892–1966)
Albert Gilbert, jeweler
For Maison Patek Philippe
Leaf Fish brooch
Paris, 1960–66
Cast and engraved yellow and grey gold
H. 6.7 cm; W. 6 cm
Gift of Madame Jean Lurçat, 2003
Inv. 2003.125.9

SNAKES and
OTHER REPTILES

The snake has always been
a rather ambiguous motif.
In many civilizations since
antiquity, it has been linked to
our primal origins, to Mother
Earth and hence to the female
sex; but it is also associated with
water and symbolizes rebirth
because of the way it regularly
sheds its skin. The negative
characteristics attributed to the
snake – cunning, evil, temptation
– conversely link it with chaos,
strife and war. In the Christian
world, the snake carries the
connotations of evil and sin.
Because of its bite, it presages
death and is thus associated
with hell and the kingdom of
the dead. It is also linked to
divination and can be seen in
depictions of the Delphic Oracle
or Pythia.

Opposite and right:
Snake bracelet
Italy, antiquity (?)
Hammered gold band
Diam. 8 cm; W. 0.5 cm
Bequest of Jeanne Marie Mosticker, 1966
Inv. 40344

Opposite, from top to bottom
and left to right:
Snake ring
France, Bourbon Restoration
Enamelled gold
Diam. 2.3 cm; W. 2 cm
Snake ring
Enamelled gold, rose-cut garnets
Diam. 2.2 cm; W. 1 cm
Gifts of Cérette Meyer, 1938
Inv. 34213 and 34216

Snake ring
France, Bourbon Restoration
Enamelled gold
Diam. 1.8 cm; W. 0.7 cm
Snake ring
Enamelled gold, cabochon turquoise
Diam. 2.2 cm; W. 0.7 cm
Bequests of Jean-Jacques Reubell, 1934
Inv. 31004 and 30755

Toi et Moi engagement ring
Paris, early 20th century
Yellow and grey gold, ruby, rose-cut
and brilliant-cut diamonds
Diam. 2.2 cm; W. 1 cm
Bequest of Jean-Jacques Reubell, 1934
Inv. 30964

Snake ring
Middle East (?), 19th century
Iron, turquoise
Diam. 2.2 cm
Gift of Jean-Jacques Reubell, 1934
Inv. 31006

Above left:
Émile Froment-Meurice (1837–1913)
Salamander of Francis I brooch
Cast and tooled silver
H. 3.5 cm; W. 4 cm
Above right:
Lizard bracelet
Silver, gilded silver, enamel
Diam. 6.5 cm; W. 2 cm
Gifts of Henri Vever, 1924
Inv. 24452 B and 24405

The shape and symbolism
of the snake make it an ideal
motif for jewelry. During the
Bourbon Restoration, snake
rings in enamelled gold were
very popular and heralded the
naturalistic decorative style
that flourished under Napoléon
III, when snakes, lizards and
salamanders were combined
with plant motifs and statements
of love.

The motif of the serpent eating its own tail – the ouroboros – is found in ancient China, Egypt and Greece. It symbolizes the cyclical nature of time and the concepts of motion, continuity and self-sufficiency. It can also represent the union of the heavens (circle) and the underworld (serpent) and therefore the connection between two opposing principles: heaven and earth, good and evil, day and night, yin and yang. In the early 19th century, it was used in jewelry as a symbol of eternal love.

Below left and centre:
Ouroboros ring
Paris, 1798–1809
Inscription: *Se rejoindre ou mourir* ('Join or die')
Gold, enamel, inscription engraved in reserve
Diam. 2 cm; bezel H 2 cm; W. 1.3 cm
Gift of Cérette Meyer, 1938
Inv. 34220

Below right:
Ouroboros bracelet with key
France, late 19th century
Gold
H. 10 cm; Diam. 6 cm
Bequest of Madame la Marquise Arconati-Visconti, 1925
Inv. 23990

Opposite, above:
Snake bracelet
Italy (?), 19th century (?)
Gold
Diam. 7 cm; W. 3 cm
Bequest of Jeanne Marie Mosticker, 1966
Inv. 40345

Opposite, below:
Jules Debut (1838–1900) and Léon Coulon (?)
Snake necklace, made in five sections
Paris, 1879–90
Gold, brilliant-cut diamonds
L. 82 cm; W. 1 cm
Gift of the Marquise Arconati-Visconti in memory of Raoul Duseigneur, 1916
Inv. 20386

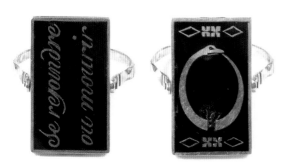

Maison Germain Bapst (1855–1921)
and Lucien Falize (1839–97)
8 Novembre 1870 bracelet maquette
Paris, 1880–92
Gold-electroplated metal
Diam. 6.2 cm; W. 3 cm
Gift of Lucien Falize, 1893
Inv. 7580

Domestic
ANIMALS

Animals were first domesticated during the Neolithic period, at a time when human beings had begun to settle in one place and to practise agriculture. The relationship between mankind and animals changed: instead of being predators, humans were now the protectors of some species. Evidence of this close relationship can be seen in amulets dating back to prehistoric times. Small animals carved from Alpine rock crystal were commonplace in the Roman world from the 1st century onwards.

Opposite and below right:
Duck amulet
Europe, 3rd–8th century
Rock crystal, cabochon garnets
H. 1.5 cm; W. 3.5 cm; Depth 2 cm
Bequest of Georges Rufin, 1934
Inv. 31461 B

Above right:
Fish amulet
Europe, 3rd–8th century
Gold, rock crystal, cabochon garnets
H. 4 cm; W. 1.6 cm; Depth 1.3 cm
Provenance unknown, pre-1933
Inv. PR 2017.14.1

Far left:
Dog ring
France, 18th or 19th century (?)
Inscription: *Soye.moy fidelle*
('Be faithful to me')
Silver, enamel
Diam. 2 cm; bezel H. 1 cm; W. 1.2 cm
Bequest of Jean-Jacques Reubell, 1934
Inv. 31073

Left:
Dog ring
Paris (?), late 18th century
Silver, enamel, old-style
brilliant-cut diamonds
Diam. 2 cm; bezel H. 3 cm; W. 1.5 cm
Gift of Cérette Meyer in memory
of her brother, 1914
Inv. 19438

Opposite, above:
Dog tie pin
France, early 19th century (?)
Gilded silver, gold, old-style
brilliant-cut diamonds
H. 4 cm; W. 2.5 cm
Gift of M. Merlin, 1892
Inv. 7088

Opposite, left:
Frédéric Boucheron (1830–1902)
Jean Menu (born 1830) and Burdy
(born 1833), jewelers
Dog's Head tie pin
Gold, sard
L. 10.5 cm; head H. 1.9 cm; W. 2 cm
Opposite, right:
Louis Aucoc (1850–1932), jeweler
Poodle tie pin
Gold, opal, matrix opal
L. 9.5 cm; head H. 1.5 cm; W. 1.5 cm
Gifts of Count Moïse de Camondo
in memory of his father Count Nissim
de Camondo, 1933
Inv. 28874 B and Inv. 28874 D

Opposite, below:
Dog's Head tie pin
England, late 19th century
Painting under glass, gold, silver,
rose-cut diamonds
L. 9 cm; W. 1.6 cm
Bequest of Jean-Jacques Reubell, 1934
Inv. 30736 D

In the Middle Ages, dogs were viewed as coarse, lewd, even unholy creatures. Their status rose when they became associated with the aristocratic pursuit of hunting and they began to be included in paintings as pets. They also featured on tombs, shown lying at the foot of their master as a symbol of fidelity, and dog motifs in 19th-century jewelry carry the same symbolism. While the idea of dogs as representing faithfulness was prevalent in the 18th and 19th centuries, the hunting motif continued to dominate on jewelry for men, with dogs often carved from hardstones or enamelled under rock crystal.

Sleeping Dog bracelet
French provinces, mid-19th century
Silver, gold, braided hair
Diam. 7 cm; W. 2.5 cm
Gift of Mademoiselle J. Magnin, 1928
Inv. 26523

Cats were domesticated by the Egyptians several millennia ago and were considered sacred throughout the Pharaonic era. In the Middle Ages, cats were seen as allied to the forces of darkness, owing to their ability to hunt at night. When the Black Death swept through Europe in the 14th century, it soon became clear that cats were better at hunting the rats that spread the disease than the ferrets specifically trained for that purpose. It was in this way that cats began to find their way back into our homes. Rendered in painted or ronde-bosse enamel, they appear most often on tie pins, cufflinks and other jewelry for men, in depictions that combine naturalism with wit.

Above left:
Louis Aucoc (1850–1932)
Cat and Mouse cufflink
Paris, c. 1900
Gold, translucent enamel painted on a matt ground
Diam. 1.6 cm; W. 3.5 cm
Gift of Henri Vever, 1924
Inv. 24500 C

Above right:
Georg Mendelsohn (1886–1955)
Igny, 1945–80
Cat ring
Enamel on copper
H. 2.3 cm; W. 2.2 cm
Gift of Michel Marq, 2000
Inv. 2000.71.10

Opposite:
Frédéric Boucheron (1830–1902)
Georges Le Saché, jeweler
Cat's Head tie pin
Paris, c. 1880
Gold, ronde-bosse enamel, cabochon emeralds
L. 8.2 cm; head H. 1.3 cm; W. 1.8 cm
Gift of Count Moïse de Camondo in memory of his father Count Nissim de Camondo, 1933
Inv. 28868 C

Whether an animal is represented in the decorative arts depends on the degree of interest with which it is viewed by a particular civilization. Seen in the ancient world as attributes of the gods, and depicted as fantastical hybrid monsters during the Renaissance, animals only began to be portrayed in their own right in the late 19th century, with the advent of naturalism. They are most often found on men's jewelry, especially tie pins, which cast an ironic gaze on man's domination of the animal kingdom. The specific meaning of a particular piece can sometimes be elusive, as in the case of this tie pin depicting a mouse perched on a fork, tempted by a pearl instead of a piece of cheese.

Opposite:
Mouse tie pin
Paris, late 19th century
Gold, enamelled cast iron, pearl
L. 8.7 cm; head H. 1.2 cm; W. 3.2 cm
Gift of Count Moïse de Camondo
in memory of his father Count Nissim
de Camondo, 1933
Inv. 28875 A

Right:
Rabbit tie pin
Paris (?), late 19th century
Gold, ronde-bosse enamel
L. 7.5 cm; head H. 1.6 cm; W. 1 cm
Bequest of Jean-Jacques Reubell, 1934
Inv. 30735 A

The malleability of some animal forms makes them particularly useful as a decorative devices. The flowing 'S' shape of a swan's or duck's neck, for example, is perfectly suited to the design of a buckle or fastening. During the Renaissance, facing pairs of bird heads were included in the published designs of Étienne Delaune among others, and were revived in the late 19th century for jewelry in the neo-Renaissance style. The motif was later given a new lease of life thanks to the discovery of Japanese art and in particular the study of sword guards, which are round ornaments, usually in openwork with a central hole, around which Japanese craftsmen arranged their chosen motifs. Fighting cockerels are given a naturalistic treatment on a number of pieces, but René Lalique interprets the same motif here in a more stylized manner.

Above:
Ducks' Heads fastener
Iran (?), 19th century
Steel inlaid with gold,
cabochon turquoises
H. 3 cm; W. 9 cm
Gift of Marguerite Arquembourg, 1956
Inv. 37888

Opposite:
René Lalique (1860–1945)
Two Cockerels pendant
Paris, c. 1901–2
Gold, enamel on gold, cabochon
star sapphire, brilliant-cut
and rose-cut diamonds
H. 6.9 cm; W. 5.1 cm
Gift of Laura Dreyfus-Barney in memory
of her sister Natalie Clifford-Barney, 1966
Inv. 40103

Valiant and watchful, the cockerel is traditionally seen as the king of the farmyard and the herald of the new day, and was associated with the sun and the sun god Apollo in antiquity. From the Romanesque period onwards, it was placed on church towers to greet the dawn and call worshippers to morning prayers. Owing to its Latin name, *gallus*, it also became the emblem of the land of Gaul, and later of the King of France and subsequently France itself, a role it still holds today. This is the proud and noble bird that Jean Lurçat's shimmering design alludes to, while Albert Duraz shifts the focus to the cockerel's armoured appearance and fighting stance.

Albert Duraz (1926–2004)
Two Cockerel clips
Lyon, 1963
Silver
Left: H. 11.5 cm; W. 4.5 cm
Right: H. 9 cm; W. 4 cm
Gifts of Albert Duraz, 1992
Inv. 992.601 and 992.602

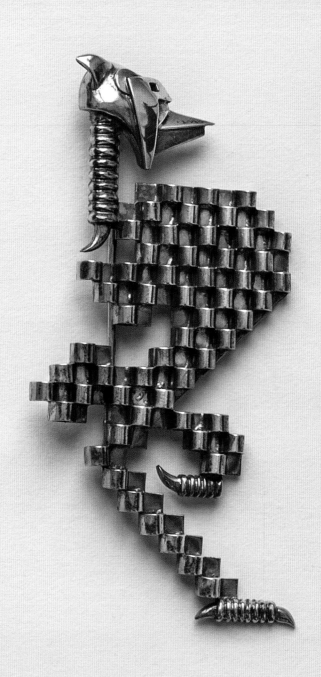

The ultimate domestic animal, vital for farming, hunting, warfare or simply as a means of transport, the horse has also long been valued for its beauty, by artists ranging from Leonardo da Vinci to Théodore Géricault, and for its symbolic significance (it was believed to accompany the soul to heaven). A wide variety of horses are featured on tie pins – plough horses, carriage horses, racehorses. They may also be reduced, metonymically, to a simple emblem of good fortune, such as a hoof, horseshoe or nail.

Below, from left to right:
Two Horses in Harness tie pin
England (?), late 19th century
Silver, gold, rose-cut diamonds
L. 8 cm; head H. 2 cm; W. 1.7 cm
Gift of Henri Vever, 1928
Inv. 26726 E

Maison Robin Frères
Horse tie pin
Paris, 1870–78
Gold
L. 10 cm; W. 3 cm
Horse's Hoof tie pin
Paris (?), late 19th century
Gold, enamel
L. 7.8 cm; W. 0.5 cm
Bequest of Jean-Jacques Reubell, 1934
Inv. 30734 A and D

Opposite:
Ibex Heads ring
Italy (?), 19th century
Gold, ronde-bosse enamel, emerald
H. 3 cm; W. 3 cm; Depth 1.1 cm
Gift of Michel Calmann in memory of his mother Madame Paul Calmann, 1936
Inv. 32537

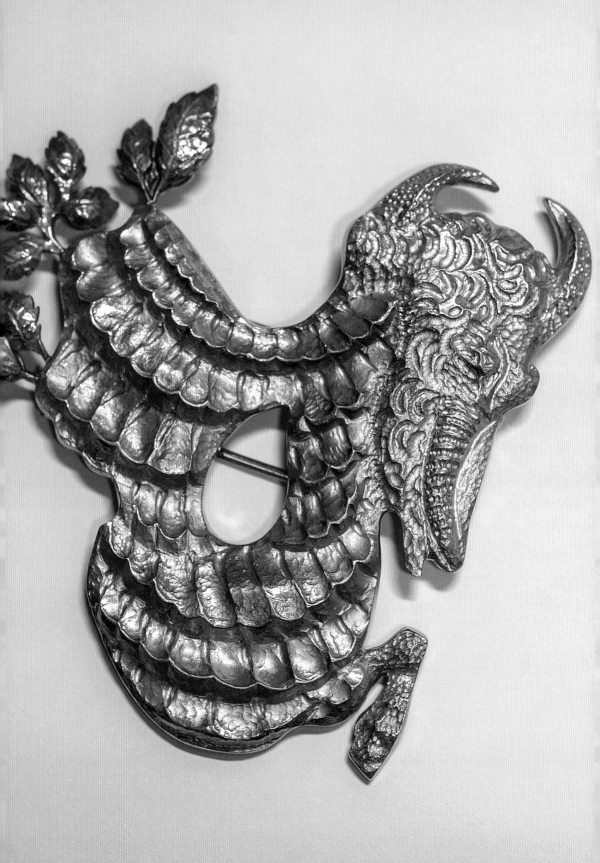

Variously depicted as a bull, bullock, cow or calf, depending on the civilization, cattle have always played an important role in both religious and daily life. The bull is the wild counterpart to the sacrificial bullock of the ancient world and the cattle associated with the Christian nativity, and it has also spawned hybrid creatures such as the Minotaur. In the 20th century, its imagery is linked to the world of bullfighting. The bull's head and hide represented on Jean Lurçat's brooch recall the Minotaur of Greek myth, while Albert Duraz's pendant is reminiscent of a tribal African mask.

Opposite:
Jean Lurçat (1892–1966)
Albert Gilbert, jeweler
For Maison Patek Philippe
Bullock brooch
Paris and Geneva, 1960–66
Gold
H. 7.2 cm; W. 6.8 cm
Gift of Madame Jean Lurçat, 2003
Inv. 2003.125.11

Above:
Albert Duraz (1926–2004)
Bull's Head pendant
Lyon, 1950
Silver
H. 7.5 cm; W. 4.5 cm
Gift of Albert Duraz, 1992
Inv. 992.595

Sheep, like cattle, may be represented in very different forms. On one hand, the ram symbolizes strength, vitality and sexual ardour; on the other, the lamb and the ewe are emblems of purity and innocence. The lamb of the New Testament is a reference to Jesus Christ, the 'Lamb of God' who offered himself as a sacrifice to expiate human sin. The Paschal lamb also reminds us of the Old Testament story of the ram sacrificed by Abraham in place of his son Isaac. In the 16th-century pendant shown opposite, it rests on a copy of the Holy Scriptures and holds the banner of the Christian faith.

Left:
Ram's Head bracelet
Italy (?), late 19th century
Gold, lapis lazuli
Diam. 6.5 cm
Gift of Jean Eugène Chevalier, 1925
(jewelry belonging to Madame
J. E. Chevalier, née E. M. Hill)
Inv. 37053

Opposite:
Paschal Lamb pendant
France (?), 16th century
Gold, enamel, baroque pearl,
natural pearls
H. 3.5 cm; W. 3 cm; Depth 1.1 cm
Bequest of Madame Ménard, 1969
Inv. 41866

Line Vautrin was an
unconventional artist.
Her jewelry designs often
incorporated a new material that
she invented herself – Talosel,
made of layers of cellulose
acetate – and she approached
her craft in a unique way that
was both witty and playful.
This necklace, in gilded bronze,
is an affectionate and ironic
interpretation of the childhood
game of leapfrog (known as
saute-mouton or 'jump-sheep'
in French) and also refers to the
age-old technique of counting
sheep in order to fall asleep.
Informal and comical, Vautrin's
jewelry introduces a note of
fun into a field where luxury
is usually a serious business.

Opposite:
Line Vautrin (1913–97)
Jumping Sheep necklace
Gilded bronze, enamel
H. 24 cm; collar diam. 13 cm
Purchased by the State and given
to the Musée des Arts Décoratifs in 2008
Inv. 2008.56.79

Wild
ANIMALS

The natural world is all that remains of our planet as it once was and perhaps of the Garden of Eden. The wild creatures that most fascinate humanity are the large mammals – whale, elephant, bear – and the big cats that embody so much graceful symmetry and power. Their attraction is all the stronger because, despite our technological progress and dominance over the animal kingdom, these creatures are still extremely dangerous to us. Wild cats are often reproduced on men's jewelry, such as this leopard's head tie pin with its striking rendering of the spotted fur.

Opposite and right:
Leopard tie pin
Paris, late 19th century
Gold, petrified palmwood,
rose-cut diamonds
L. 8.9 cm; head H. 1.8 cm; W. 1.6 cm
Gift of Count Moïse de Camondo
in memory of his father Count Nissim
de Camondo, 1933
Inv. 28874 C

Opposite:
Alphonse Fouquet (1828–1911)
Lions belt buckle
Cast, tooled and matted silver
H. 9 cm; W. 15 cm
Gift of the artist, 1908
Inv. 14851 G

Above left:
Georg Mendelsohn (1886–1955)
Lion pendant
c. 1950
Enamel on copper
H. 5.5 cm; W. 2.8 cm
Gift of Michel Marq, 2000
Inv. 2000.71.2

Above right:
Castellani
Lion of St Mark pendant
Rome, c. 1875–81
Gold, mosaic glass
Diam. 2.3 cm
Bequest of Madame la Baronne
Nathaniel de Rothschild, 1901
Inv. 9848 A

Since antiquity, the lion has been considered a symbol of strength and power via a parade of gods and heroes who succeeded in vanquishing the beast in single combat. During the Middle Ages, the lion was hailed as king of the beasts, taking the place of the bear, which the Church regarded as too pagan. In heraldry, it is often shown 'rampant', rearing up on its hind legs with open jaws, a bristling mane and a protruding tongue. The lion is also the emblem of St Mark the Evangelist, patron saint of Venice, and appears in this guise on a mosaic glass pendant with a gold ground – one of many similar designs by the Italian firm Castellani – that echoes the motifs found on the walls of St Mark's Basilica in Venice.

As men's clothing grew more standardized during the Industrial Revolution, eventually leading to the 'men in suits' who still populate the business world today, ornament – and therefore jewelry – became increasingly rare in the male wardrobe. Until the end of the 18th century, accessories, ribbons, embroidery and jewelry were seen as signs of power and wealth when worn by men, but in the modern era, mainstream male adornment is generally restricted to a handful of discreet elements: buttons, watches, cufflinks, pins. As if to underline this display of 'manliness', animal motifs on men's jewelry – as seen in these examples – tended to make references to hunting or other tests of strength (bear, boar, dog), with the occasional touch of wit (monkey).

Below:
Camel tie pin
Paris (?), late 19th century
Inscription: *Coût 25 louis* ('Price: 25 louis')
Cast and tooled gold, enamel
L. 7.4 cm; head H. 1.6 cm; W. 2.6 cm
Inv. 28875 D

Opposite, from top to bottom:
Bear's Head tie pin
England (?), 19th century
Baroque pearl, gilded silver, rubies,
rose-cut diamonds
L. 6.5 cm; head H. 2.5 cm; W. 2 cm
Inv. 28870 E

Maison Paul et Henri Vever
Monkey's Head tie pin
Paris, late 19th century
Gold, labradorite, opaque enamel,
rose-cut diamonds
L. 9 cm; head H. 2 cm; W. 1 cm
Inv. 26726 F

Boar's Head tie pin
Paris, late 19th century
Gold, labradorite, ruby, sapphire,
rose-cut diamonds
L. 8.5 cm; head H. 1.4 cm; W. 2.2 cm
Gifts of Count Moïse de Camondo
in memory of his father Count Nissim
de Camondo, 1933
Inv. 28874 A

Monkey Drinker tie pin
Paris, late 19th century
Gold, cast and tooled silver
L. 6.8 cm; W. 0.8 cm
Bequest of Jean-Jacques Reubell, 1934
Inv. 30735 E

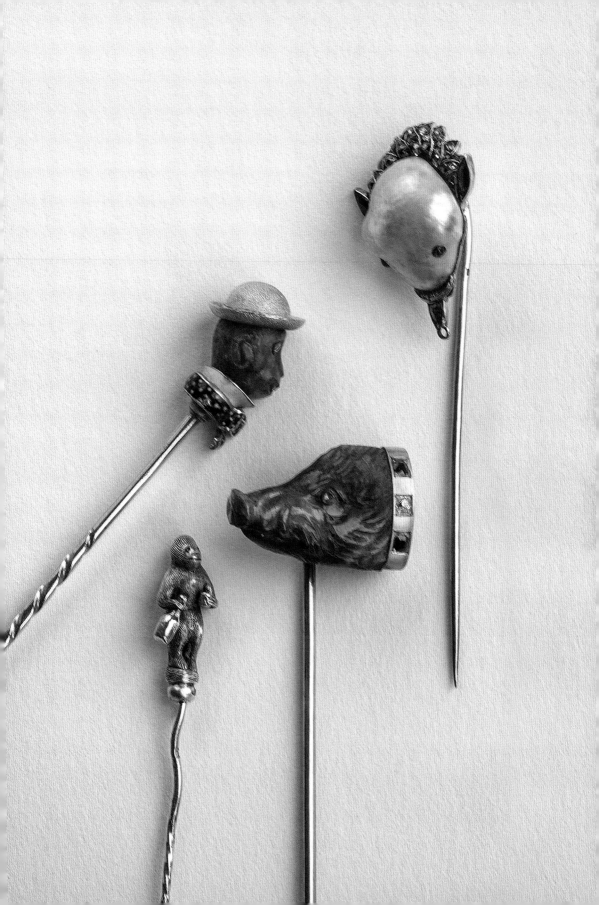

Mythical
BEASTS

The ancient civilizations of the Mediterranean produced a vast menagerie of imaginary creatures. Greek mythology abounds in human hybrids such as centaurs, fauns and Gorgons, as well as fantastic beasts – chimeras, griffins, sphinxes, dragons and hydras. During the Renaissance, the unusual shapes of baroque pearls were often used to depict these creatures. Decorative compositions of the 17th and 18th centuries surrounded them with grotesques and arabesques. In the late 19th century, monstrous forms were revived in the decorative arts displayed at the Paris Exposition Universelle in 1878 and 1889, later leading to the butterfly women and flower women of Art Nouveau.

Opposite and right:
Henri Nocq (1868–1942)
Dragon pendant
Paris, c. 1895
Gilded silver, enamel, glass
H. 8 cm; W. 4 cm
Gift of Max Polack in memory
of Henri Nocq, 1943
Inv. 35110

In medieval French legend, the guivre (or vouivre) was an undulating serpent with a dragon's head. It was generally represented either swallowing or spitting out a human figure, sometimes a child. This fantastical dragon-like beast was a popular heraldic device in the Middle Ages, as attested by the arms of the Visconti family in Florence and here the Arconati-Visconti family arms. The creature originated in legends that were common in eastern France, the Jura region and Switzerland. The motif of the swallowed child comes from a folk tale from the Franche-Comté area in the 18th century: one night, a selfish and spiteful widow decided to steal a treasure belonging to the guivre, who had picked up her sleeping child and carried it away. To punish the woman, the guivre kept the child – the woman's most precious 'possession' – but returned it a year later after the woman had mended her ways and become a kinder and more generous person.

Top:
Maison Germain Bapst (1855–1921)
and Lucien Falize (1839–97)
Guivre brooch modelled
on the Arconati-Visconti family arms
Paris, 1880–92
Gold, enamel
Diam. 3.5 cm; Depth 2 cm
Gift of the Marchioness Arconati-Visconti
in memory of Raoul Duseigneur, 1916
Inv. 20384

Above:
Maison Germain Bapst (1855–1921)
and Lucien Falize (1839–97) (?)
Guivre brooch modelled
on the Arconati-Visconti family arms
Paris, 1880–92
Gold, enamel
H. 2.5 cm; W. 2.5 cm
Gift of the Marchioness Arconati-Visconti
in memory of Raoul Duseigneur, 1916
Inv. 20376

Perhaps the best known of mythological beasts, the dragon was once associated with the creation of the world; it was a violent primitive creature that the gods had to vanquish before they could rule the earth. In Christian symbolism, the dragon is associated with Lucifer; the Archangel Michael and St George are both depicted as defeating the dragon in the name of God. In East Asian cultures, the dragon is an emblem of power and good fortune. These late 19th-century tie pins make good use of its sinuous shape and reflect the eclecticism of the period, combining medieval influences with the contemporary Japoniste style.

Right:
Dragon tie pin
Paris, 1878–89
Gold, Colombian emerald, cabochon
rubies, rose-cut diamonds
L. 8.4 cm; head H. 2.5 cm; W. 1.4 cm
Gift of Count Moïse de Camondo
in memory of his father Count Nissim
de Camondo, 1933
Inv. 28871 F

Far right:
Louis Wièse (1852–1923)
Dragon tie pin
Paris, c. 1890
Gold, matt ronde-bosse enamel
L. 7 cm; head diam. 1.1 cm
Gift of Jean-Eugène Chevalier, 1925
Inv. 37064

Lucien Falize (1839–97)
Birds purse fastening
Paris, c. 1890
Cast, tooled and gilded silver
H. 8.6 cm; W. 5.2 cm; Depth 1.4 cm
Gift of the Marchioness Arconati-Visconti
in memory of Raoul Duseigneur, 1916
Inv. 20362

In Greek mythology, the chimera was a hybrid monster with the head and body of a lion, a goat's head growing from its back and a serpent as its tail. The creature was regarded as female and was sometimes depicted with a woman's head and breasts on a lion's body. There is no classical myth that refers to a fight between a chimera and a snake, but it was a scene often represented in Renaissance-inspired works of the 19th century. Many other fantastical creatures have been created by fusing monsters from the ancient world.

Opposite:
Dogs' Heads ring
Paris, 19th century
Gold, pearl
H. 3.5 cm; Diam. 2 cm
Bequest of Jean-Jacques Reubell, 1934
Inv. 30866

Above right:
Émile Froment-Meurice (1837–1913)
Phoenix brooch
Paris, 1878–1900
Gold, cast and tooled silver
H. 5 cm; W. 3 cm
Gift of Henri Vever, 1924
Inv. 24476

Below right:
Louis Wièse (1852–1923)
Chimera and Serpent brooch
Paris, 1878–1900
Tooled silver openwork
H. 2.5 cm; W. 4.5 cm
Gift of Jean-Eugène Chevalier, 1925
Inv. 37050

In China and Japan, two stylized lion statues are often placed at the entrance to a temple as guardians. Sometimes known collectively as 'Lions of Fo', the right-hand one is generally male, and shown with a ball under his paw, while the one on the left is female and accompanied by one of her cubs. In Japan, the lion-dog or *koma-inu* ('Korean dog') is a hybrid beast with a single horn on its head. Its role is to instil fear and protect the entrances to homes and sacred places. These figures, regularly reproduced on *netsuke*, are depicted standing upright. They are rare in French jewelry, but the tie pin on the left is an exception. The motif and the techniques used to produce it are entirely Japanese.

Left:
Fantastical Japanese Figure tie pin
Paris, 1878–90
Gold, silver, copper patinated
in the Japanese style
L. 9.1 cm; head H. 4.2 cm; W. 1.6 cm
Gift of Count Moïse de Camondo
in memory of his father Count Nissim
de Camondo, 1933
Inv. 28875 C

Opposite:
Louis Wièse (1852–1923)
Lions of Fo fastening
Cast and tooled silver, moonstones
H. 4.5 cm; W. 10 cm
Gift of Jean-Eugène Chevalier, 1925
(jewelry belonging
to Madame J. E. Chevalier, née E. M. Hill)
Inv. 37023

The griffin is a fabulous creature derived from Assyrian myth, with the head and wings of an eagle and the body and tail of a lion. Its forefeet are sometimes depicted as eagle claws, sometimes as lion paws. Because it unites the earth (lion) and the heavens (eagle), the griffin is well equipped to hunt serpents and basilisks, which were regarded as embodiments of evil, and symbolizes the union of strength and intelligence. The griffin is frequently depicted in Byzantine and Italian textiles, and also in the gold- and silverwork of the Middle Ages and the Renaissance. In jewelry, the griffin motif reappeared in the late 19th century via the Renaissance revival, in copies of classical pieces by the Italian firm Castellani and in the chatelaines designed by Alphonse Fouquet.

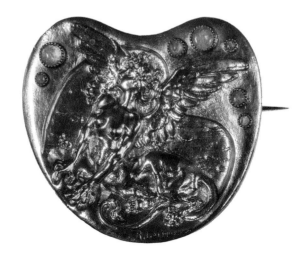

The sphinx has the body of a lion, a human head and the wings of a bird. In Egyptian iconography it is generally male, but in Greek mythology it is female, and associated with the story of Oedipus. The artist Gustave Moreau painted *Oedipus and the Sphinx* in 1864 and the Greek sphinx subsequently became a popular motif for the rest of the 19th century. Like embodiments of Time or the Seasons, it provides an ideal decorative motif for a chatelaine.

Above:
René Lalique (1860–1945)
Sphinx brooch
Paris, 1893
Partially gilded silver, cabochon opals
H. 3.7 cm; W. 4 cm
Gift of Henri Vever, 1924
Inv. 24518 B

Opposite:
Alphonse Fouquet (1828–1911)
Sphinx chatelaine with watch
Paris, 1878
Cast, tooled and engraved gold
H. 11 cm; W. 5 cm
Gift of the artist, 1908
Inv. 14851 F

Jean Lurçat (1892–1966)
Albert Gilbert, jeweler
For Maison Patek Philippe
Two Cockerels necklace
Paris and Geneva, c. 1960
Gold
L. 28.5 cm; W. 7 cm
Gift of Madame Jean Lurçat, 2003
Inv. 2003.125.5

SELECTED BIBLIOGRAPHY

G. P. Philomneste (Gabriel Peignot), *Amusemens philologiques ou Variétés en tous genres,* Paris, A. A. Renouard, 1808

Henri Vever, *French Jewelry of the 19th Century* (1906–8), London: Thames & Hudson, 2001

Georges Fouquet (ed.), *La Bijouterie, la joaillerie, la bijouterie fantaisie au XXe siècle*, Paris, 1934

Guido Gregorietti, *Jewelry Through the Ages*, New York: Simon & Schuster, 1969

J. Anderson Black, *A History of Jewels*, London: Orbis Books, 1974

Jean Lanllier and Marie-Anne Pini, *Five Centuries of Jewelry in the West*, New York: Leon Amiel, 1983

Barbara Cartlidge, *Twentieth-Century Jewelry*, New York: Harry N. Abrams, 1985

Hugh Tait, *Seven Thousand Years of Jewellery*, London: British Museum, 1986

A. Kenneth Snowman (ed.), *The Master Jewelers*, London: Thames & Hudson, 1990

Deanna Farneti Cera (ed.), *Jewels of Fantasy: Costume Jewelry of the 20th Century*, New York: Harry N. Abrams, 1992

Line Vautrin and Patrick Mauriès, *Line Vautrin: Sculptor, Jeweler, Magician*, London: Thames & Hudson, 1992

Deanna Farneti Cera, *Amazing Gems: An Illustrated Guide to the World's Most Dazzling Costume Jewelry*, New York: Harry N. Abrams, 1997

Marguerite de Cerval (ed.), *Dictionnaire international du bijou*, Paris: Éditions du Regard, 1998

Monique Poulenc and Anne-Michèle Margerie, *Les Bijoux traditionnels français*, Paris: Réunion des Musées Nationaux, 1998

Katherine Purcell, *Falize: A Dynasty of Jewelers*, London: Thames & Hudson, 1999

Dominique Forest and Évelyne Possémé, *The Jewelry Collection of the Musée des Arts Décoratifs, Paris*, Paris: Union Centrale des Arts Décoratifs, 2002

Godelieve and Patrick Sigal, *Les Paruriers, bijoux de la haute couture*, Brussels: Fonds Mercator, 2006

Diana Scarisbrick, *Le Grand Frisson. Bijoux de sentiment de la Renaissance à nos jours*, Paris: Textuel, 2008

Laurence Mouillefarine and Évelyne Possémé (eds.), *Art Deco Jewelry: Modernist Masterworks and Their Makers*, London: Thames & Hudson, 2009

Animal, exhibition catalogue, Paris: Musée des Arts Décoratifs, 2010

Opposite:
Eagle's Claw tie pin
Paris, late 19th century
Gold, lapis lazuli
L. 10 cm; W. 1.8 cm
Bequest of Jean-Jacques Reubell, 1934
Inv. 30665 C

Right:
Alphonse Fouquet (1828–1911)
Chimera Fighting the Serpent, maquette for a necklace
Paris, Exposition Universelle, 1889
Plaster and wax
H. 17 cm; W. 14.5 cm; Depth 5 cm
Gift of Monsieur and Madame Jean Fouquet, 1958
Inv. 38112

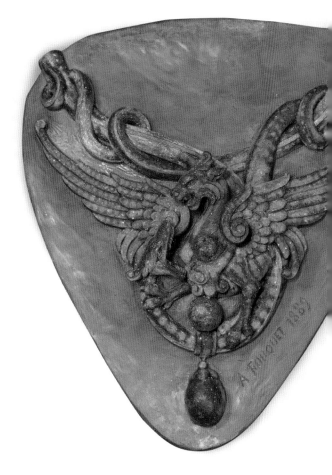

Translated from the French *Faune: Galerie des Bijoux* by Ruth Sharman.
Photographs by Jean-Marie del Moral,
except pages 31 left, 36, 49 and 91
(photographs by Jean Tholance)

First published in the United Kingdom in 2017
by Thames & Hudson Ltd, 181A High Holborn, London WC1V 7QX

www.thamesandhudson.com

First published in the United States of America in 2017
by Thames & Hudson Inc., 500 Fifth Avenue, New York, New York 10110

www.thamesandhudsonusa.com

Original edition © Les Arts Décoratifs, Paris 2017
This edition © 2017 Thames & Hudson Ltd, London

British Library Cataloguing-in-Publication Data
A catalogue record for this book is available from the British Library

Library of Congress Control Number 2017934854

ISBN: 978-0-500-51998-1

Printed and bound in Italy